Want free goodies?
Email us at freebies@honeybadgercoloring.com

@honeybadgercoloring

Honey Badger Coloring

Shop our other books at
www.honeybadgercoloring.com

Wholesale distribution through Ingram Content Group
www.ingramcontent.com/publishers/distribution/wholesale

For questions and customer service, email us at
support@honeybadgercoloring.com

© Honey Badger Coloring. All rights reserved. No part of this publication
may be reproduced, distributed, or transmitted, in any form or by any means, including
photocopying, recording, or other electronic or mechanical methods, without prior
written permission of the publisher, except in the case of brief quotations embodied
in critical reviews and certain other noncommercial uses permitted by copyright law.

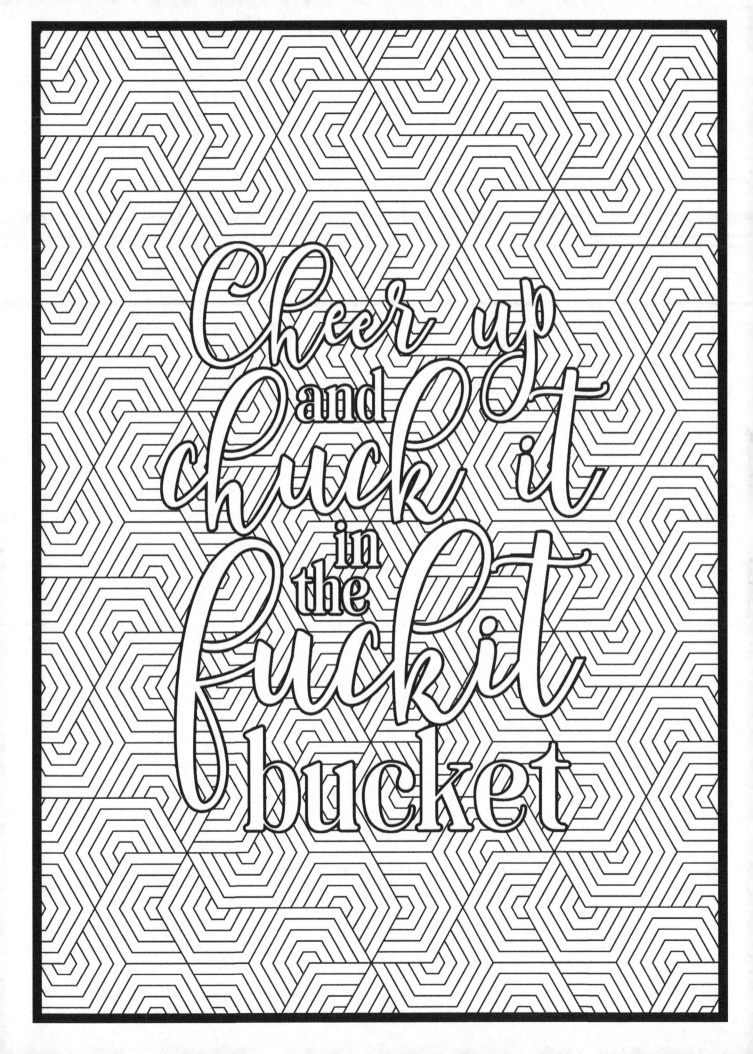

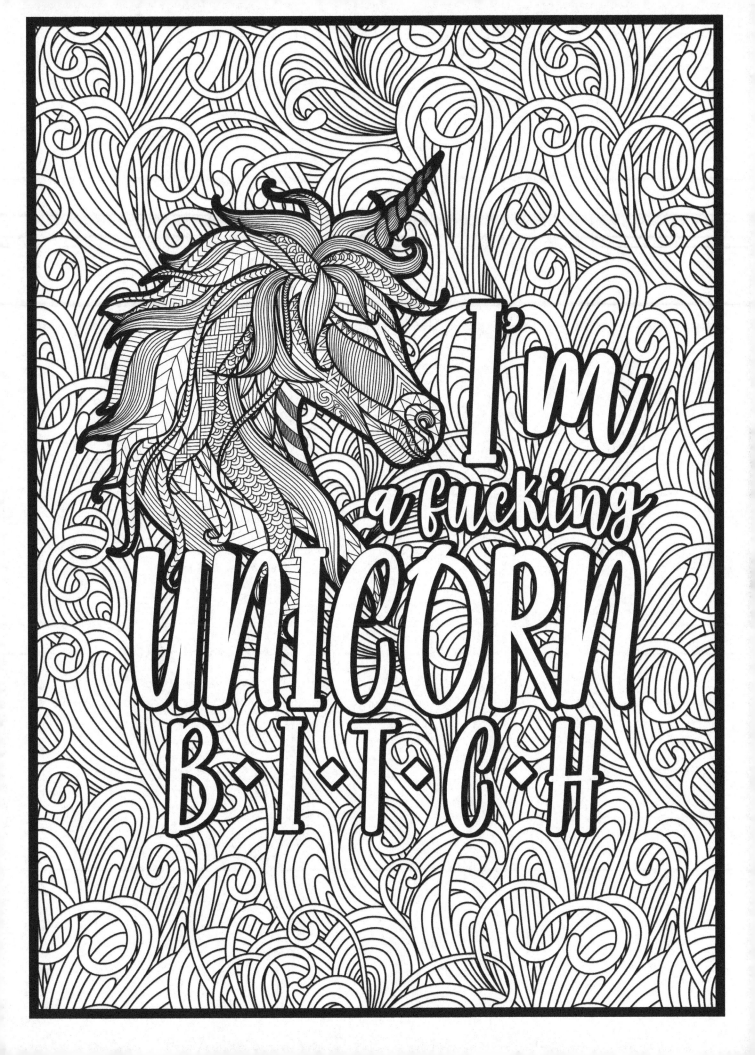

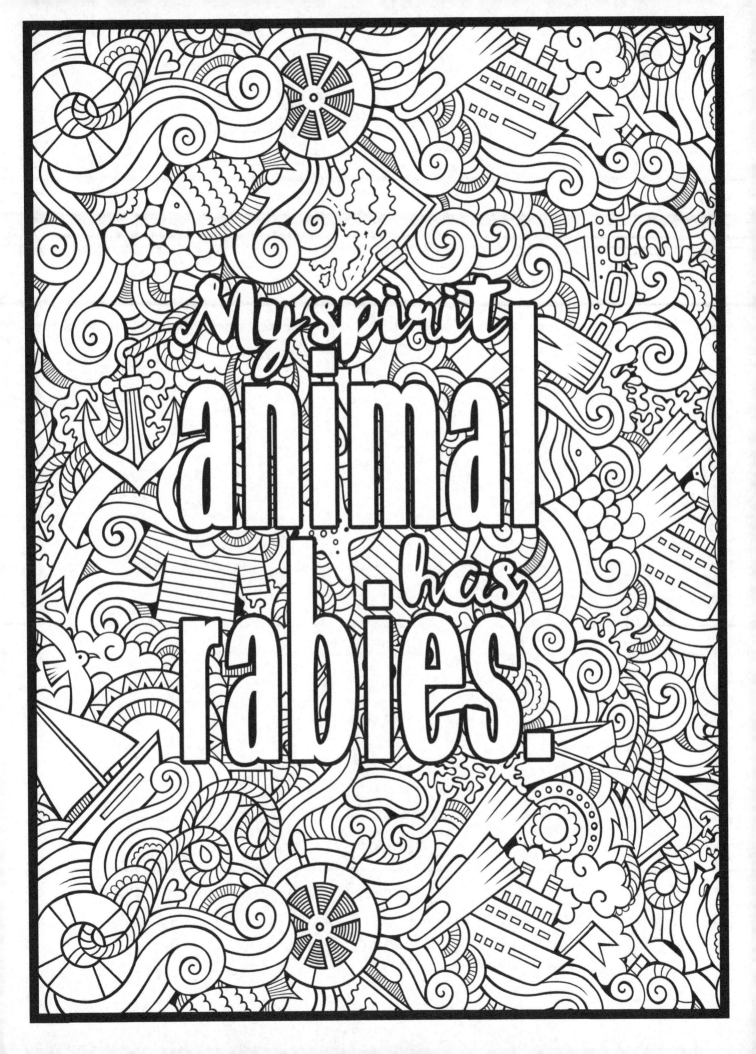

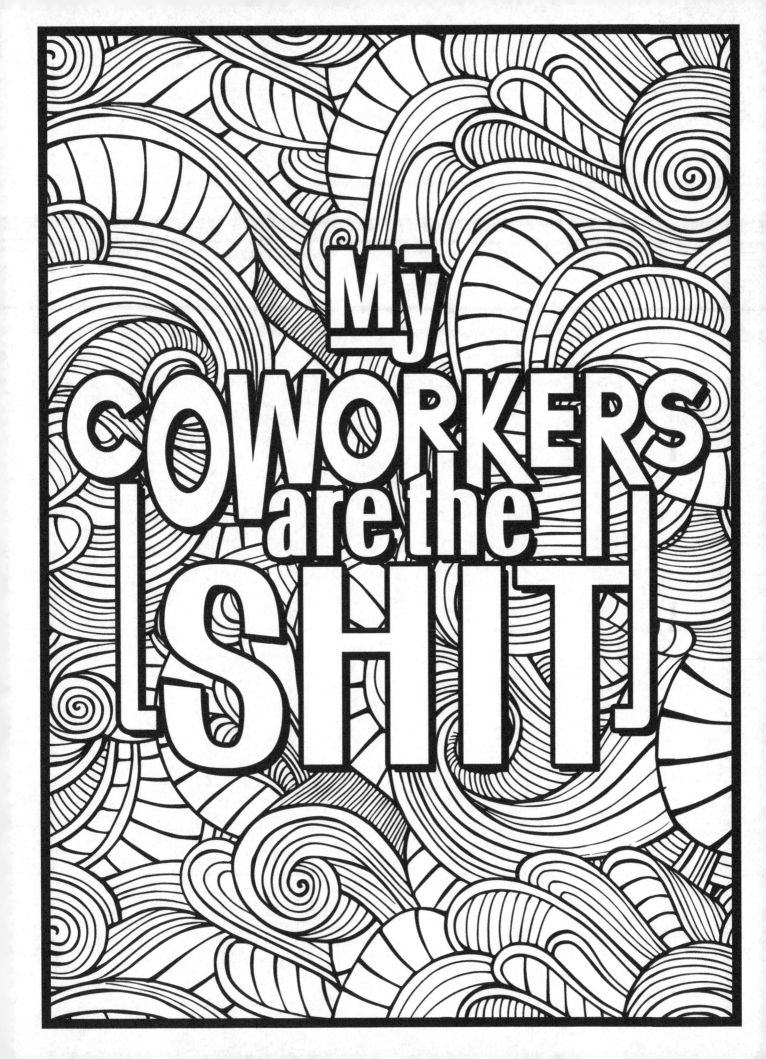

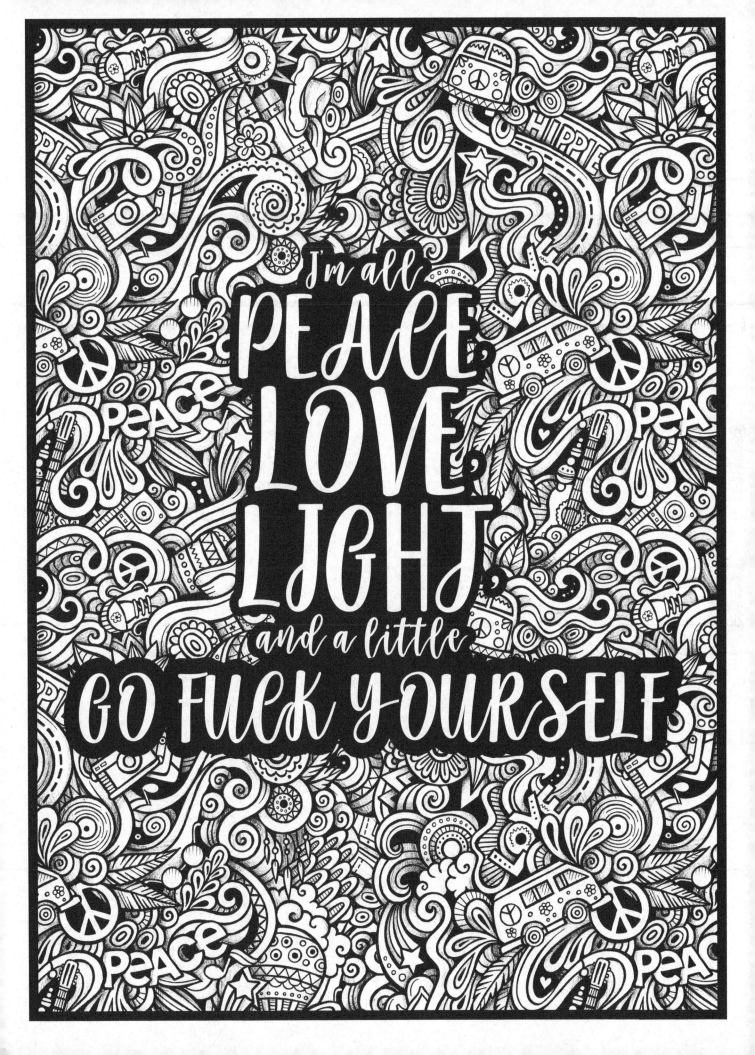

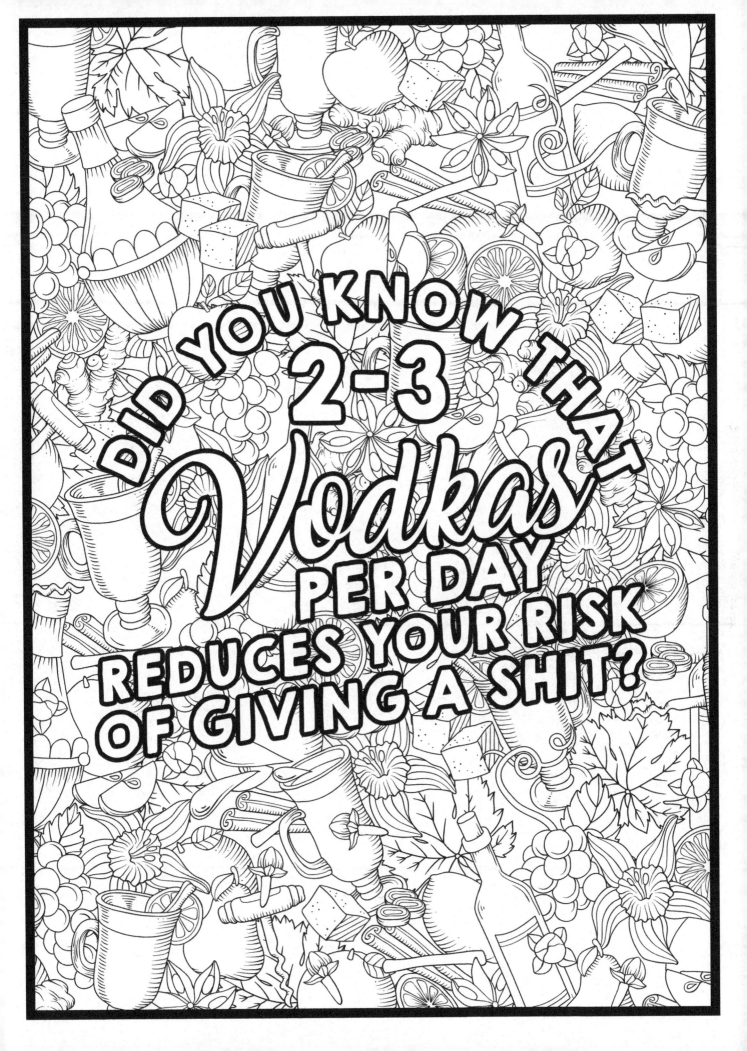

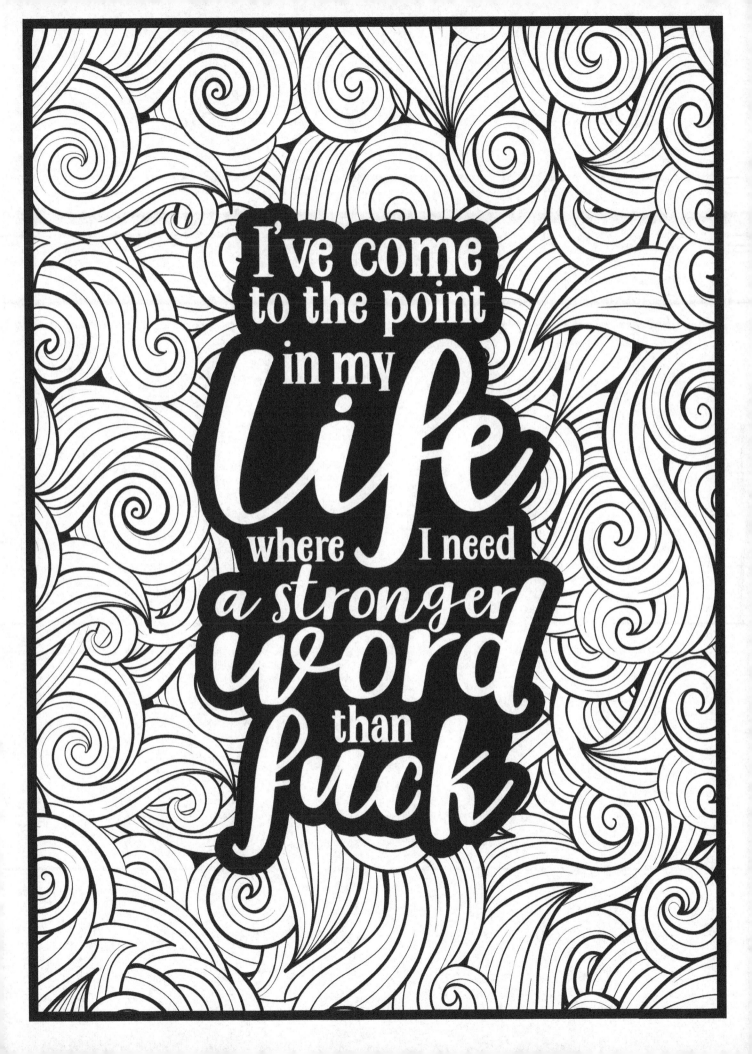

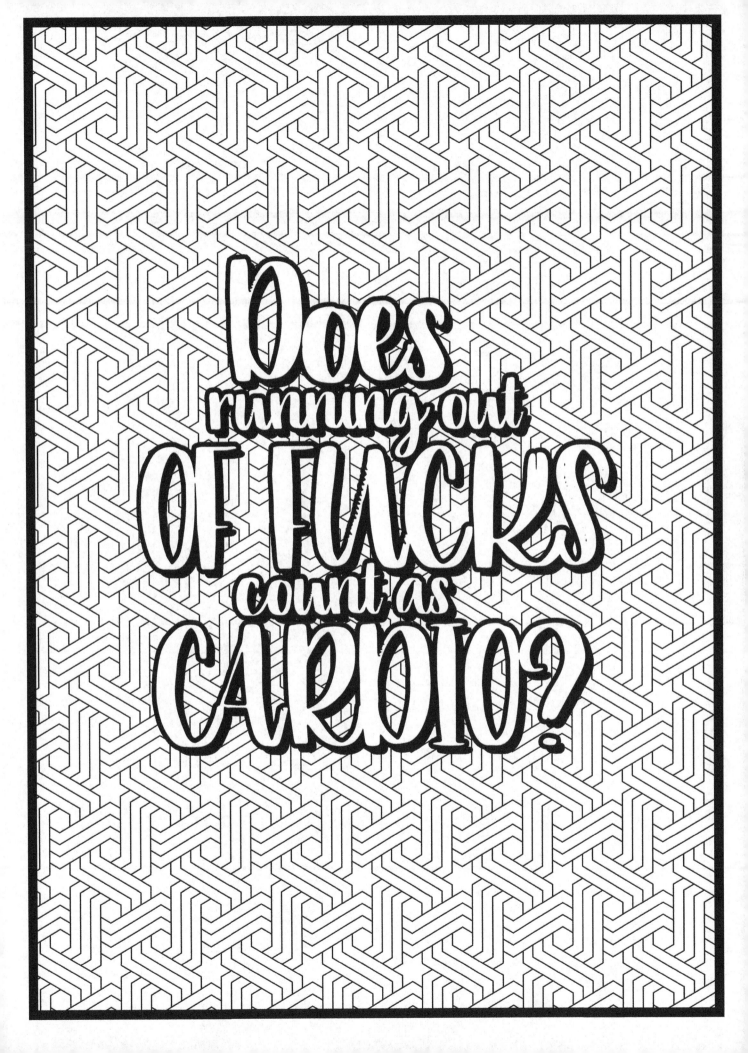

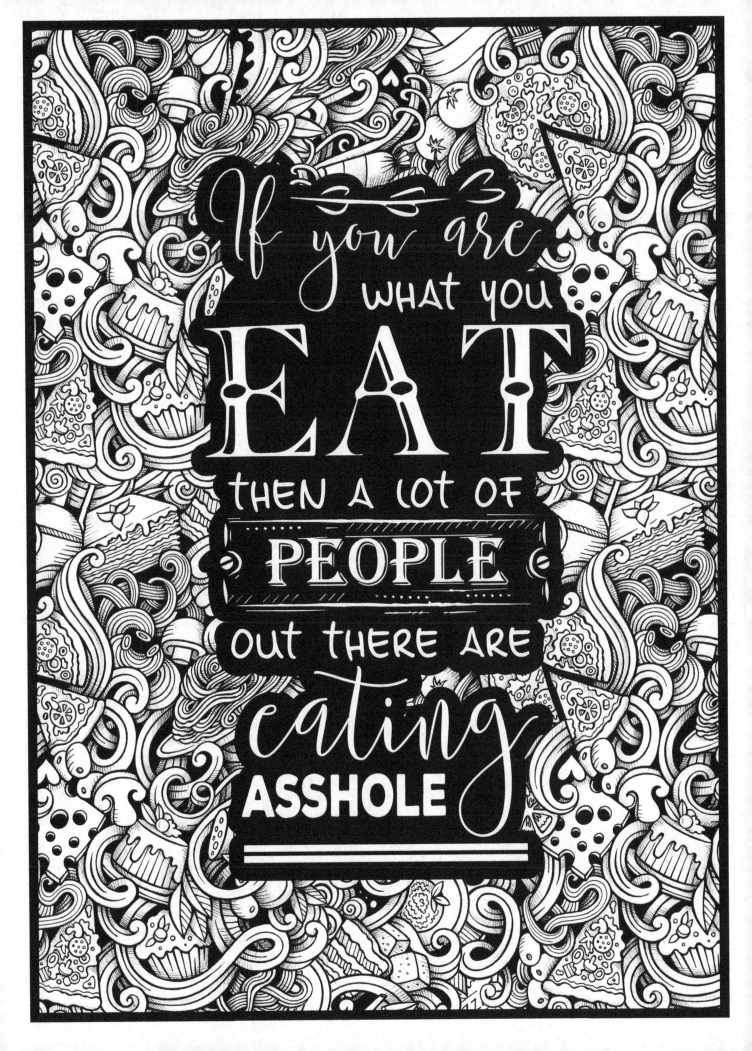

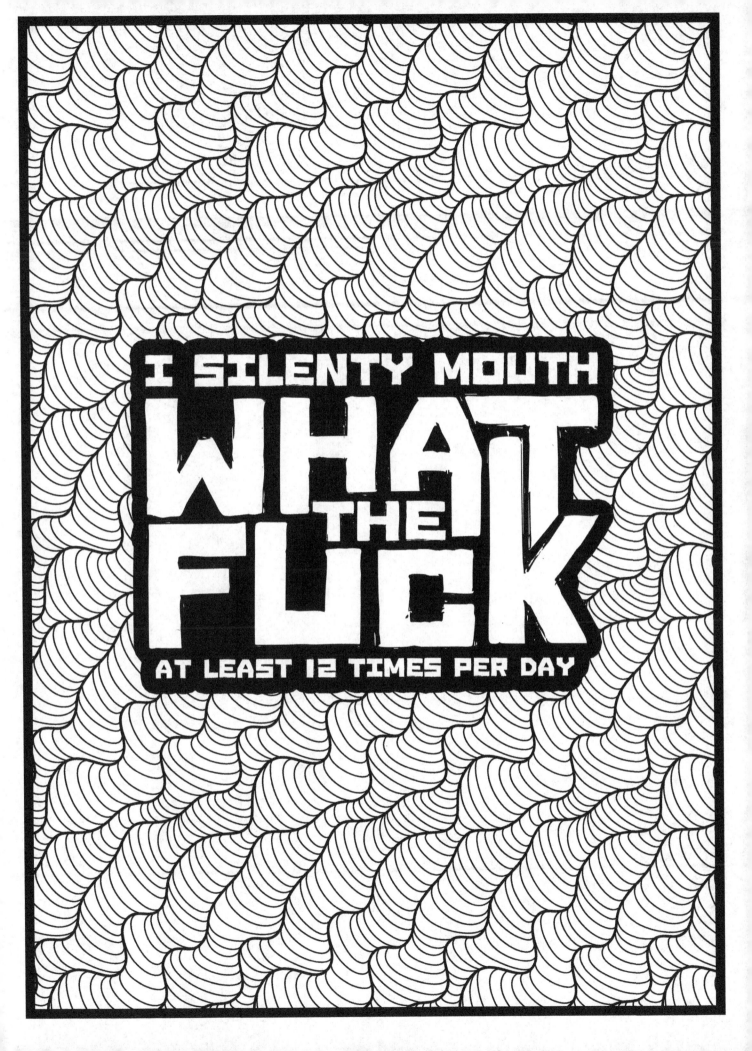

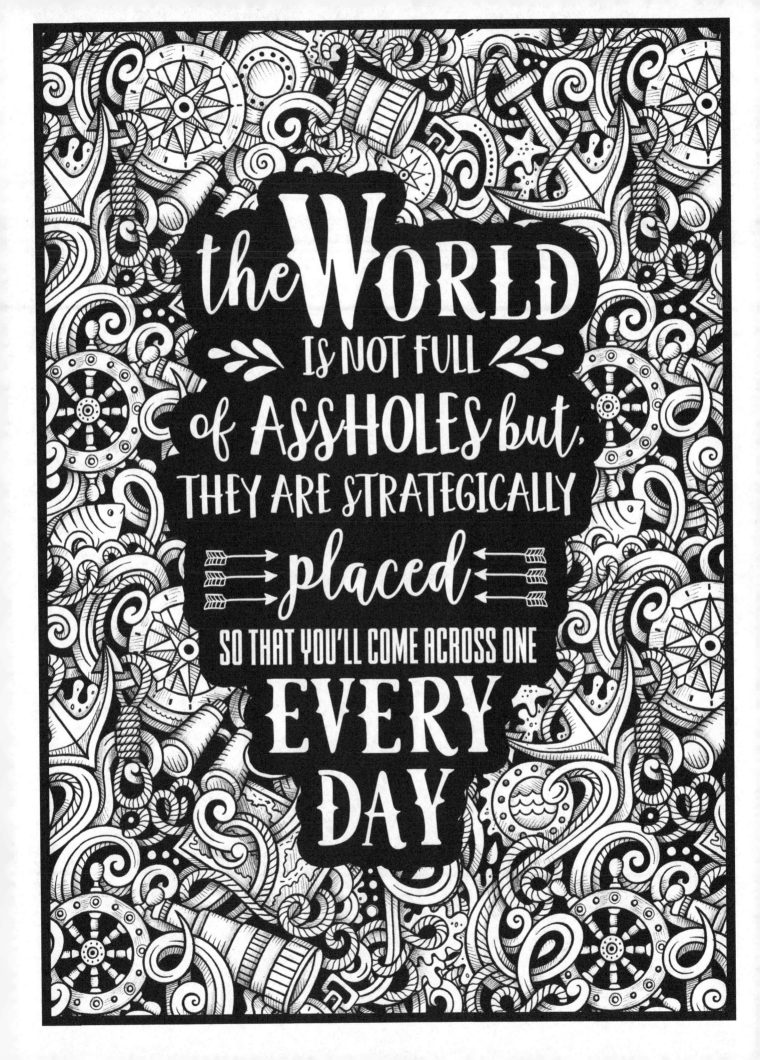

I am a nice PERSON, Just don't PUSH my BITCH button.

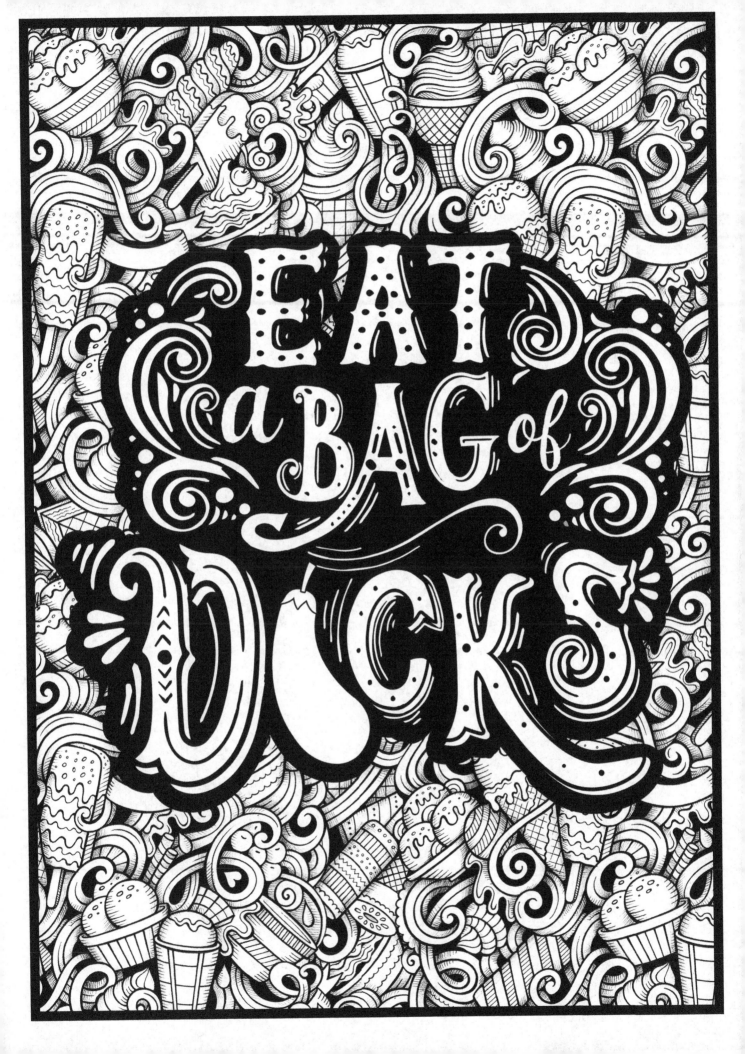

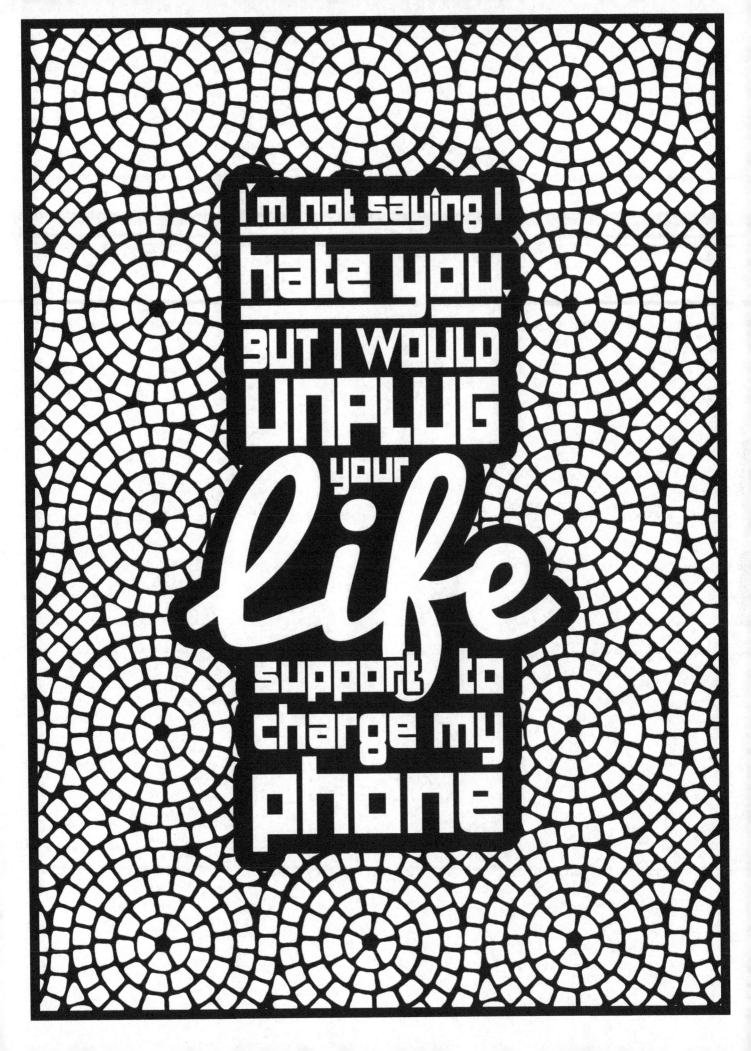

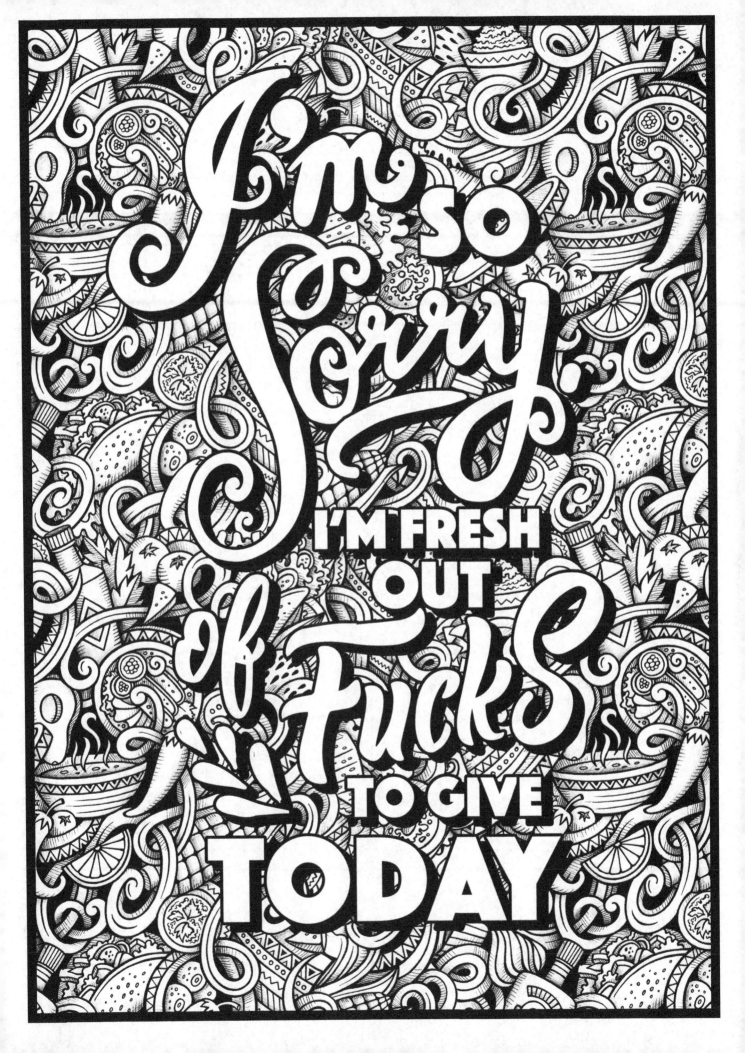

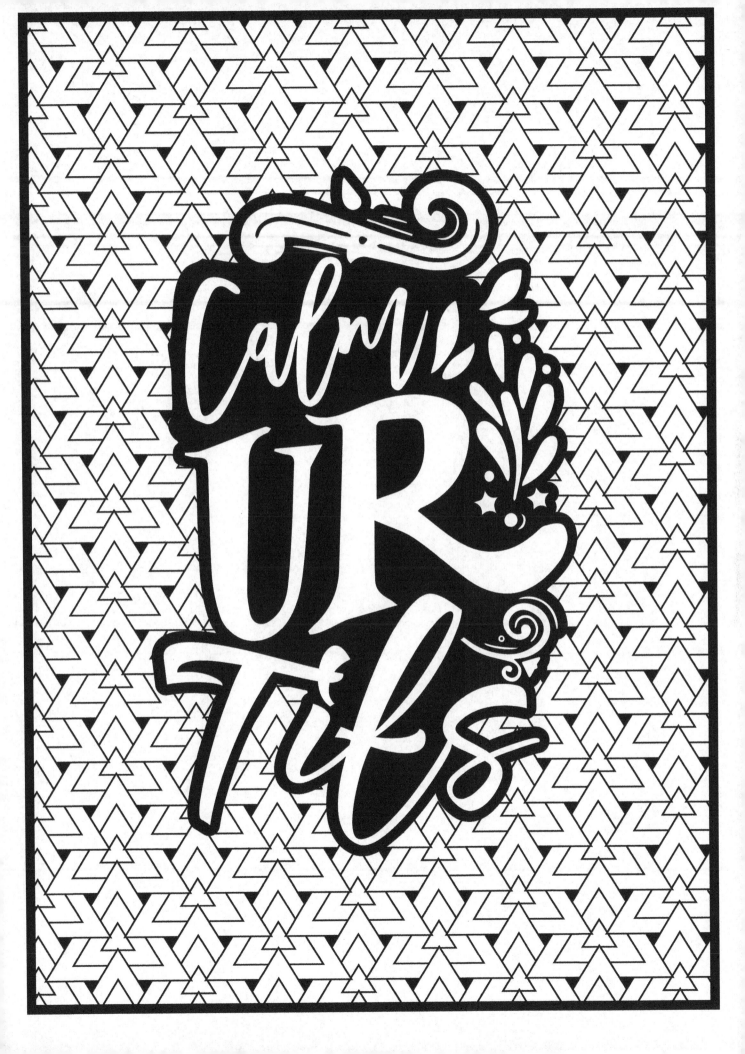

WORLD'S *Okayest* SOCIAL WORKER

Want free goodies?
Email us at freebies@honeybadgercoloring.com

@honeybadgercoloring

Honey Badger Coloring

Shop our other books at
www.honeybadgercoloring.com

Wholesale distribution through Ingram Content Group
www.ingramcontent.com/publishers/distribution/wholesale

For questions and customer service, email us at
support@honeybadgercoloring.com